FRIENDING GOD

FRIENDING GOD

Social Media, Spirituality and Community

ANTONIO SPADARO, S.J.

Translated by
Robert H. Hopcke

A Crossroad Book
The Crossroad Publishing Company

The Crossroad Publishing Company
www.CrossroadPublishing.com
© 2016 by Antonio Spadaro, S.J.

Book design by The HK Scriptorium

Library of Congress Cataloging-in-Publication Data
available from the Library of Congress.

ISBN 978-0-8245-2214-8

Books published by The Crossroad Publishing Company may be purchased at special quantity discount rates for classes and institutional use. For information, please e-mail sales@CrossroadPublishing.com.

Contents

Contents

Introduction

Once upon a time, there was the compass, a clever little instrument used to figure out where you were heading geographically. It was invented by the Chinese in ancient times and brought to Europe in the twelfth century. But beyond the literal compass, in those olden times, we also had, as it were, our own sort of interior compass, which pointed us toward the religious world as the source of all meaning. Like the needle on a physical compass, this interior compass of ours pointed naturally and unmistakably in one direction and one direction only: toward God. God was the north. So, if the compass we had did not point north, that was surely because there was something wrong with the compass itself and obviously not because the north didn't exist. But then, beginning around the Second World War, we started using radar, which was able to determine the location of objects both stationary and moving. Radar would scan the environment and indicate the location of even the faintest signal, though it could not show the precise direction in which that object was moving.

Nowadays, a new cultural metaphor has taken hold, in the form of a question: "Where are you, God?" We understand ourselves to be seekers after God, looking for a message that we each deeply need to hear, exemplified by *Waiting for Godot* and so many other similar works of literature throughout the twentieth century. We have become "hearers of the word"—to use theologian Karl Rahner's notable expression that theologically recasts the technological image of radar—in search of a message.

And today? Are these symbols still valid? The truth is, though still vivid and in some way accurate, these symbols of the compass and of radar are less powerful, for we go about living our lives these days no longer asking God too many questions. In an era post-compass and post-radar, we find ourselves having become, in a way, decoders, that is to say, engaged in a system of accessing and deconstructing questions of meaning on the basis of a multiplicity of possible answers that present themselves to us without our really having to seek them out. In fact, we spend our lives bombarded with messages all the time; so our current problem is not how to pick up a meaningful signal but rather how to make sense of the messages we get, how to recognize their relative importance and their meanings against a background of multiple, possible answers.

Consequently, today, what's important is not to find an answer. Everyone's got an answer! Rather, the important thing is to recognize what the significant questions are, which questions are fundamental, and thus, to make an opening in our lives through which God may still speak to us.

1

Spiritual Technology

We the people of the twenty-first century are creatures of the World Wide Web, always online, always connected, always communicating. And we—like all others throughout history—have created this technology in our own image, which gives this creation of ours a spiritual dimension as well. The Church knows the truth of this well, and it has known it for a long time. One crucial moment in understanding the spiritual dimension of new technologies was the promulgation by the Second Vatican Council of the statement *Inter mirifica,* on December 4, 1963, which starts with the following proclamation:

Among the wonderful technological discoveries which men of talent, especially in the present era, have made with God's help, the Church welcomes and promotes with special interest those which have a most direct relation to men's minds and which have uncovered new avenues of communicating most readily news, views and teachings of every sort.

A few months later, in 1964, with reference to the technological research center of the Aloisianum in Gallarate, Pope Paul VI would use words that were, in my opinion, prophetic and disturbingly beautiful. At a time when many of our major electronics already existed in use but when the personal computer, smartphone, and especially the Internet were as yet beyond even imagining, the center at Gallarate was at work creating a computer-based analysis of St. Thomas Aquinas's *Summa theologiae* and the Bible. About these priest-scientists, the Pope said:

Science and technology, once again brothers, have offered us once again a wonder, and at the same time, have given us a glimpse of new mysteries. But what is sufficient for

us . . . is to note how this very modern con-
venience may be made available to our culture; how this mechanical brain may assist
our spiritual mind; and though expressed
in its own language of thought, it seems
yet to enjoy a certain dependence upon us.
Have you not begun to apply its findings
to the Latin Bible? And what have they
shown? Has the sacred text been reduced
to any other common piece of writing, to
be played with by amazing, to be sure, but
ultimately automated, mechanical means?
Or is not your effort to imbue these
mechanical instruments with a spiritual
function, to ennoble them and lift them
up into service, such that they may touch
the sacred? Is it the spirit which is made
prisoner in matter, or is it not that matter,
already tamed and obliged to carry out the
laws of the spirit, might offer to our very
spirit a reverence sublime? Is this the place
where our Christian ears hear the groans
of which St. Paul speaks (Romans 8:22),
of natural creatures aspiring to a superior
level of spirituality?[1]

This Pope then clearly heard arise from *homo technologicus* a groan of aspiration toward a higher level of spirituality. Our technological being is our spiritual being, and if this was true in 1964, it is even more true now that our world has been transformed into a World Wide Web.

The key point is this: there is an undeniable, profound, and radical connection between technology and spirituality. Obviously, the character of all technology is fundamentally equivocal, since our free will can be used for good or for ill, but it is precisely this possibility that connects technology to our spiritual life, for it is one of many common means that we have at our disposal to indeed express our spiritual nature. This notion was taken up in 2011 by Benedict XVI, who said of the new technologies: "If used wisely, they can contribute to the satisfaction of the desire for meaning, truth, and unity which remain the most profound aspirations of each human being,"[2] and who then went on to state further in his encyclical *Caritas in veritate* (2009) that the digital age is "a profoundly human reality, linked to the autonomy and freedom of man. In technology we express and confirm the hegemony of the spirit over matter."[3] Technology is an expression of our capacity to organize matter according to a framework of primarily spiritual values, such that Christians are, therefore, called to understand its deeper nature, the vocation that digital technologies have in relation to the life of the spirit.

Technological development, when understood correctly, succeeds therefore in expressing our longing for "transcendence" of the human condition and the life we actually live day to day. The same can be said of "cyberspace" as well. Catholic theologian Tom Beaudoin has noted, in fact, how what we have come to call cyberspace, known for the speed of its connections, is an apt representation of our desire for an even greater wholeness, a greater presence to one another, an even greater level of knowledge:

Cyberspace highlights our own finitude. ... Yet, it also mirrors our desire for the infinite, the divine. Given the direction in which technology is moving, cyberspace

15

seems increasingly omniscient and omni-present, which may be what the obsession with speed is all about theologically. To search for this fullness of presence, one that spans and unites the human and divine, is to operate in the field of a divine–human experience, in which spirituality and technology intersect.[4]

The believer is called to accomplish a task: to hold applied scientific research not as a "means" (which would reduce these tools to mere "gadgets") nor as expressions of a "will to power" (which would turn these tools into "weapons"), but rather to use this science to answer God's call to form and to transform creation. This is what Pope John Paul II was hoping for when he spoke of a "divinization" of the entirety of human ingenuity.[5]

2

The Web and Relationships

Until a few years ago, "technology" was a term synonymous with progress, automation, and industrial-economic development and had little or nothing to do with the concept of friendship or the experience of relationship. Nowadays, however, the decisive and far-reaching impact technology has had on human relationships in general is a manifest given and must be acknowledged. Despite its propensity to foster an experience of alienation, the Internet is also an environment that allows people to experiment with new forms of personal expression, contact, and relationships. We have come to call the "places" where these activities take place collectively the "social network," precisely because it is about the communications between the people that frequent them. Moreover, even with regard to content, the Internet itself has evolved. No longer do we simply publish our own personal "pages," but the content we put out presumes that others will participate interactively with this content, such that the very term "publication" has come to mean participation and sharing.

A particular social network platform—like Facebook, Twitter, YouTube, LinkedIn, Pinterest, and others—is made up of a group of people connected, generally speaking, by common interests, open to sharing ideas and knowledge, as well as parts of their lives; and they do so by sharing links to websites they find interesting, as well as by posting their own personal photos and videos. In other words, the social network consists of ordinary people, not engineers or experts, who are sharing content that is relevant to their own lives and their own interests, making full use of this participatory technology, which is easy to access and costs virtually nothing to enjoy.

There are, however, various hidden dangers. The risk that these platforms might become the property of a small group of corporations whose sole interest is profit is not at all an unrealistic fear to have. The first and most notorious step in this direction was the acquisition of You-Tube by Google for $1.65 billion in 2006 and then, more recently, the acquisition of Whats-app by Facebook in 2014 at the hefty price of $19 billion. Thus, the Internet has become, in fact, big business. Nevertheless, recent history also shows us that if and when a particular platform becomes purely profit driven, it begins to forfeit the trust of its users who waste no time leaving it behind to go elsewhere.

And, of course, there is also the problem of privacy. Social networking sites are full of sensitive data about the people who use them, and it is amply clear that the level of personal privacy one has online is, in many ways, relative—not to mention the ways in which advertising, pornography, and violence are all easily posted online and presented in ways make them all at least palatable, if not seductively attractive.

Beyond these specific examples of risks and dangers, though, the overall shift in attitudes and concepts of relationship due to the Internet is striking:

The new digital technologies are, indeed, bringing about fundamental shifts in patterns of communication and human relationships. These changes are particularly evident among those young people who have grown up with the new technologies and are at home in a digital world that often seems quite foreign to those of us who, as adults, have had to learn to understand and appreciate the opportunities it has to offer for communications.[1]

We all know well the level of suspicion with which computer-based technologies and their impact on society are viewed by many, and the level of confusion—the steep "learning curve," if you will—that the Internet has created for all of us. And yet, in and of themselves, these new information technologies are a gift of extraordinary potential. They invite us to expand our horizons and to listen to the deeper desires in our heart, which we can now go online to express.

To acknowledge this gift, therefore, is the only valid premise by which we might live and proclaim our faith in a time of digital media: we need to recognize the value of these media, their spiritual "capacity," and to see how they hold within them an answer to a "call." And yet, in an age in which technology is becoming the very fabric of human connection and knowledge, it is necessary to ask ourselves: can we live out the Gospel online? The answer seems, decisively, yes.

3

The Internet Is a Real Place

The Internet is not simply an ensemble of cables, signals, modems, and computers, and it would be a mistake to identify the "reality" and the experience of the Internet with the technological infrastructure that makes it possible. That would be like confusing one's family's "home" with the structure, the "house," that one inhabits.

Above all things, the Internet is an experience, an experience in which the cables and signals make one feel "at home" in the way one's parents and relatives make one feel at home. It is therefore, a real "space," a place that becomes more and more organically integrated into our everyday lives: a new existential context.

One of my African students at the Pontifical Gregorian University once said to me: "I love my computer because *inside* my computer are all the friends I have in Africa." This was true: in his computer were Facebook, Skype, Twitter, all the various means by which he could stay in contact with his friends living elsewhere. His "community" was real, thanks to the Internet, and his simple statement makes us reflect on the fact that the digital world has had an impact on the very meaning of our existence itself.

Our life is there, in the photos and thoughts that we share: there are our friends. In a way, online, we come to see that we exist. A part of the life we live has, indeed, become digital. It is as if the Internet has at this point become the "connective tissue" through which we express not only our identity but our very "presence." And such futuristic reflections, surprisingly, lead us far back into history, back to our very origins; for, while times and technology may change, the nature of what it means to be human stays the same, as do our basic needs, and among the most essential of these is "to live somewhere," to be "present" in a place, to be in conversation.[1]

All of this suggests that, even from this point of view, the experience technology provides us is not at all alien to what it means to be authentically human. The Internet is "revolutionary," that is true, but it is a revolution with firm roots in the past that builds up ancient ways of transmitting knowledge and living together in civil society, one that evokes memories, that gives shape to instinctive desires. So dazzled are we by its novelty, perhaps, our capacity for reflection may not have matured sufficiently to appreciate how the brilliant innovations brought forth by the Internet are not relevant to just the present or the future to come, but in fact also give place and form to elements of our collective past, our nostalgic desires, the expression of eternal human values, as well. These technologies carry our fundamental desire as human beings to connect with one another, our desire to communicate, that desire for friendship which is so deeply rooted in our nature.

The Internet is not just a "tool" for communication that one can pick up or put down;

it is, rather, an "environment," a culture, one that determines a new way of thinking, that creates new fields of exploration and education, that contributes to stimulating our intelligence, creating knowledge and structuring our relationships in new ways. Because we are not immune to evolving in the way we manipulate our environment, in the process of transforming our means of communication, we, too, and our culture are transformed as well.

But what are the particular characteristics of this place we call the Internet? Above all, it is a real place, and do the encounters that occur there truly take place between real people. Cyberspace is not unreal, fictional, or merely virtual, but rather a true extension of our real, everyday lives which demands of us a sense of "responsibility and truthfulness."[2]

Here is one of the major challenges: the distinction between real and virtual, which many frankly insist on making, does not exist. Between the physical and digital, there may be, at most, two different modes of human "presence," which have an important and practical consequence: to maintain an on(line)/off(line) dualism can only increase alienation. As long as one thinks and speaks as if one needs to leave behind online relationships in order to pursue real relationships, one reinforces the schizophrenia of a generation that treats the digital environment as "somewhere else," merely a play space where one can create a second self, adopt an alternative identity to live a shallow life of ephemeral banality within a bubble that has no physical reality or true connection with the world or with others, an environment that, in the end, is both false and inhuman: false in the strict sense of "deceptive," since one lives there as if it weren't real though it is; and inhuman, since its comprehensive mendacity impoverishes and falsifies all human relationships that one has there.

4

Faith and Knowledge
in the Age of the Internet

The Internet, therefore, has a real effect on our experience and a true impact on what we think and how we live. The 2012 Synod on the New Evangelization recognized, among the many challenges posed by these new communications media, one fundamental "scenario" that Christians nowadays are called to understand, since, as it is put in the *Lineamenta*, "Today, no place in the world is beyond reach and, consequently, unaffected by the media and digital culture, which is fast becoming the 'forum' of public life and social interaction."[1]

In *Instrumentum laboris*, this observation is taken up again, and it is noted further that:

In acting upon people's lives, the processes made possible by the technologies of these new media have come to transform the very nature of reality. They have a direct impact upon people's experience and allow for an expansion of human potential. Our perceptions of ourselves, of others, indeed, of the world have become dependent upon the effect they exercise upon us.[2]

It thus behooves us to remember at all times that the Internet is a part of the environment we live in and that it provides an opportunity for us to develop a particular area of our capacity to experience the world. It is hardly inappropriate, therefore, to say that, with regard to evangelization, the Internet ought well to be treated like any other area of human life and culture.

Perhaps the time has come to take some further steps in this direction. I have in mind here the notion that the Internet, with all its powerful metaphors that work upon our intelligence and our imagination, might mirror the call and text of the Bible and provide a mode for understanding the Church and our communion of faith, the nature of revelation, the liturgy, the sacraments. In short, the Internet is the locus for all the traditional areas of study within our systematic theology. Reflection is important, because it enables us to acknowledge more and more how the Internet contributes to the construction of people's religious identity, in a way that has recently come to be called "cybertheology."

Cybertheological reflection is a form of knowledge that arises from reflection upon faith experience, and it is genuinely theological in the sense of the formula *fides quaerens intellectum* (faith seeking understanding). So, cybertheology is not a sociological perception of Internet religiosity but is rather the fruit of a faith from which an impulse toward greater knowledge has sprung at a time when the structure of the Internet affects how we think, know, communicate, and live.

Nor it is enough to think about cybertheological reflection as simply one more of many examples of "contextual theology," that is, a theology that pertains merely to the human context in which it comes to be expressed, for,

as has been noted already, it is not at all easy
to determine what precisely the social context
of the Internet actually is (nor is it likely to
become any easier any time soon), as the world
of cyberspace becomes ever more integrated
into the ebb and flow of our everyday lives.

Pertinent here are various theological considerations I have made in other works,[2] but for
the moment, I would like turn our attention
to the particular pastoral challenges before us,
starting from the basic premise that the culture
of cyberspace challenges our capacity to formu-
late and hear a symbolic language that speaks
to the possibilities and signs of transcendence
in our lives.

In his homily on Pentecost 2012, Benedict
XVI posed an important and urgent question:
"It is true, we have increased the possibility of
communication, of obtaining information, of
transmitting news, but can we say that our ability to understand one another has increased?
Or, perhaps, paradoxically, do we understand
one another less and less?"[3] It is a question of
meaning that we might well characterize as
radical: is simply expanding the sheer volume

of our connections to others enough to foster reciprocal understanding between people and to create relationships of true communion with one another?

5

Not Just Connections
but Communion

This, therefore, is the particular task of a Catholic in the era of social networks: to grow the Internet as a place of "connection" more fully into a place of "communion." The danger of our time is precisely to confuse these two terms. Connection by itself is not enough to make the Internet a place where we share ourselves fully as human beings. To work toward this kind of sharing is the particular task of the Christian these days, and one key element in this task lies in the very character of "friendship" online.

We need to be cognizant at all times of how the Internet is modifying the very notion of who is our "neighbor," and even more specifically who is our "friend." The need to know and to be known is a deep need of ours, but the fulfillment of this need can easily be frustrated if we confuse superficial and transient contacts with true friendship, if we mistake genuine communication with exhibitionism, or if we let our healthy thirst for knowledge degrade into mere voyeurism. All the various social-networking platforms available to us represent potential aids to fuller relationships as well as threats to the same. It would be a sad thing if our desire to sustain and expand our online friendships came at the cost of making ourselves less available for face-to-face relationships born of encountering others in the course of our "real" lives: family, friends, neighbors, everyone we meet in our everyday lives at work, school, or in our free time. Social networking, paradoxically, can get in the way of real social interaction, and in this way, the Internet is and continues to be a challenge, the best response to which ought to be our commitment to always seek out the "whole person," at all times, even online.

The Church is naturally present wherever people develop their capacity for knowledge and relationship; in both its proclamation of the Good News and in its communion of faith, it provides two fundamental principles of our being and, for this very reason, the Internet and the Church are two realities destined "from the beginning" to confront each other. The challenge, therefore, is not how we should "use" the Internet, as one often hears, but rather how to "live well" in the Internet age. In this sense, the Internet is not a new "means" of evangelization, but is actually first and foremost a context in which we are called to express our faith—not just simply by showing up but rather through a Christian faith that we live connaturally in relationship to our fellow human beings.

These days, everyone is connected to everyone else thanks to social networks like Facebook or Twitter. As has been noted, such social networks as well as search engines like Google collect and keep all kinds of data on their users and then use this information to answer questions or update our contacts. It is as if Google or Facebook "knows" us through the way we have accessed the

Web, through the sites we visit, through what we have shown interest in. The inherent risk here is that I become enclosed in a sort of "bubble" that filters out everything and everyone different from me, such that I am no longer aware of people, articles, books, or research findings that do not already correspond to my own preconceived ideas or that express opinions that differ from my own, until in the end, I am surrounded by a world of information and relationships that look like me and reflect only me.

The danger in this is obvious: one risks becoming closed off to the intellectual challenges that are provided by diversity and otherness. To lose sight of what is different, to shut oneself up against what is new or unexpected outside of my predetermined relational or mental frameworks is to foster intolerance. Here, more than ever, dialogue between people of different faiths or lifestyles, ecumenism, interreligious dialogue, as well between groups and movements within the Church, assumes an even greater value in a world where it is easy to create, especially on the Internet—despite all of its ostensible openness—islands of self-referentiality.

It is necessary to say here that to create the communion of faith that Catholics experience in the Church, communication—even beautiful, healthy, good communication—is not enough. The Church is not the fruit of "consensus," that is, a "product" of mere communication. Whatever similarities there may be between the Internet and the Church end, however, on the threshold of the "vertical" dimension of the latter, which mediates not just between people but above all between heaven and earth. What needs to be kept very clear from the Catholic point of view is that the reality of the Church is principally and fundamentally "external," whereas the Web can be seen as a sort of big, self-referential text that we ourselves have written, and written in one dimension alone, the "horizontal"; with neither roots nor branches, it is a closed system.[1]

Relationships on the Internet depend on the availability and effectiveness of various tools for communication. The Church, on the other hand, cannot be reduced to a single public space, a "town hall" where people get together in the name of Christ in a network of immanent relationships, nor can it be conceived as an encyclopedic project à la Wikipedia, the fruit of many people of good will creating a "surplus" of knowledge.[2] The Church is instead a place where people are called and where this vocation goes beyond the limits of a pure and simple need to get together.

The "con-vocation" to be a part of the Body of Christ which is the Church cannot therefore be reduced to a sociological model and especially, from the Catholic point of view, it is much more than mere "networking." Rather "it designates the assembly of those whom God's Word 'convokes,' that is, gathers together to form the People of God, and who themselves, nourished with the Body of Christ, become the Body of Christ."[3] Being part of the Church comes from a foundational reality external to oneself, that is, from Jesus Christ who, through the Holy Spirit, unites himself intimately with all his faithful. It is he who binds the Church to himself in an eternal covenant and sanctifies it (Ephesians 5:26). The communion of faith is essentially a "gift" of the Spirit. Christ has in fact "shared with us his Spirit who, existing as one and the same being in the Head and in the members, gives life to, unifies, and moves through the whole body."[4] It is this gift, in the end, that—accompanied and elevated by our own good will and our actions in the world, including the Internet—transforms connection into communion.

Within the context of the Church, what "surplus" there is becomes sanctified through the action of the Spirit, which gives life to the members of the mystical body. The dynamic element of the Church, which makes it much more than just the sums of its parts, is indeed the Holy Spirit. So, while online relationships depend on the availability and effective functioning of various tools of communication, the Church as a communion of faith is fundamentally a "gift" of the Spirit, and so all communicative action in the Church derives from and has its foundation in this gift.

6

The Place of the Gift

Recent Popes have offered some very insight-ful thoughts from a Christian point of view about how our natural desire to be "close" to others might transform simple connections into a communion that goes beyond the limits of technology and the dominant cultural para-digm. Benedict XVI, in his extraordinary Mes-sage for the 43rd World Communications Day in 2009, which we have already quoted, shines the light of the biblical message on this funda-mental human desire stimulated in a new way by the new technologies. It is a desire, he writes, that "should be seen primarily as a reflection of our participation in the communicative and unifying love of God, who desires to make of all humanity one family. When we find ourselves drawn toward other people, when we want to know more about them and make ourselves known to them, we are responding to God's call—a call that is imprinted in our nature as beings created in the image and likeness of God, the God of communication and communion."[1]

Such an affirmation is important in the way that it directly connects the transformation brought about by social networking via the Internet to God's call for all humanity to become one family, and it discerns in the meaning of the Web not an abstraction but something that the Pope recognizes as essential to our humanity. The Internet is not meant to flatten the world into uniformity but instead to enable connections with one another across differences, to open dialogue, to make people feel more united one with another.

With a perspective that is even more specific, using the family as an exemplar for human society as a whole, not just as its basic unit, Pope Francis addressed the same subject in his Message for World Communication Day in 2015. In the following extended passage from his statement, we see how key the family is in his way of thinking:

Today the modern media, which are an essential part of life for young people in particular, can be both a help and a hindrance to communication in and between families. . . . The media can help communication when they enable people to share their stories, to stay in contact with distant friends, to thank others or to seek their forgiveness, and to open the door to new encounters. By growing daily in our awareness of the vital importance of encountering others, these "new possibilities," we will employ technology wisely, rather than letting ourselves be dominated by it. . . .

The family, in conclusion, is not a subject of debate or a terrain for ideological skirmishes. Rather, it is an environment in which we learn to communicate in an experience of closeness, a setting where communication takes place, a "communicating community." The family is a community which provides help, which celebrates life and is fruitful. Once we realize this, we will once more be able to see how the family continues to be a rich human resource, as opposed to a problem or an institution in crisis. At times the media can tend to present the family as a kind of abstract model which has to be accepted or rejected, defended or attacked, rather than as a living reality. Or else a grounds for ideological clashes rather than as a setting where we can all learn what it means to communicate in a love received and returned. Relating our experiences means realizing that our lives are bound together as a single reality, that our voices are many, and that each is unique.[2]

Using Francis's thoughts, in which the family is seen as a paradigm for correct communication—a story of "love received and returned," we might also see the family as a model for how to understand the online world of social networking. Like the family, the Web, too, is a place of "gift." Within terms like *file sharing, free software, open source, creative commons, user-generated content,* and *social network* there is the implication of "gift," though in different ways—and not just "gift," but the implication of a free "exchange" made possible and meaningful by forms of reciprocity that become "profitable" for those who play by the rules of this exchange, those who "take" advantage of these possibilities.

In the Christian way of thinking, though, a gift is not "taken" but is rather "received" within the context of a relationship without which it cannot happen. Grace is not free; quite the contrary, to quote Dietrich Bonhoeffer, grace is "costly." A gift creates "bonds"; its nature is that of communion. True gift carries within it, at least implicitly, the potential to create relationship, in contrast to the logic of the marketplace, which at most generates an exchange of goods or money. A gift is a gesture that has at its heart the experience of relationship. In the family, giving coincides with relatedness: giving is freely offered out of love and care.

This does not mean that a general and widespread sharing is wrong-headed or bad, but it is important to grasp that a Christian way of thinking encompasses more. Giving, as practiced on the Internet, leads to "sharing," to "solidarity," to "cooperation," all of which generosity can remain anonymous. Giving as "grace," however, insists instead on *personal relationship*, which is necessary and of which the family is the first and most eloquent social exemplar. In a family, everyone counts; everyone is our neighbor; everyone takes part in the relationship.

Here is where—with regard to our theme—a fundamental question for Christians comes into play. On the Internet, where everyone is equally close and distant and where the goods we share with one another are both immaterial (made up, though they may be, of bits and bytes) and extrinsic to ourselves—who then is our "neighbor"?

Addressing himself to an audience of communicators, Pope Francis called the power of the media "neighborliness":

"And who is my neighbor?" (Luke 10:29). This question can help us to see communication in terms of "neighborliness." We might paraphrase the question in this way: How can we be "neighborly" in our use of the communications media and in the new environment created by digital technology? I find an answer in the parable of the Good Samaritan, which is also a parable about communication. Those who communicate, in effect, become neighbors. The Good Samaritan not only draws nearer to the man he finds half dead on the side of the road; he takes responsibility for him. Jesus shifts our understanding: it is not just about seeing the other as someone like myself, but of the ability to make myself like the other. Communication is really about realizing that we are all human beings, children of God. I like seeing this power of communication as "neighborliness."[3]

7

Who Is Our Neighbor Online?

The true problem at the heart of this question is the shift that has occurred in the idea of "presence" (and thus of "neighborliness") in an age when digital media and social networks have created a form of virtual presence. What does it mean to be present to one another? One's "virtual" existence seems to be based on a rather unclear ontological principle: unencumbered by physical presence, we offer others online, instead, in sometimes very striking ways, a social presence. This social presence is, of course, not just a product of one's consciousness, a mental image, but neither is it a *res extensa*, something that possesses an ordinary, objective reality since it only happens in the course of interaction. Indeed, the spheres of existence involved in one's online presence are perhaps best understood through how they are interwoven. And what opens before us when we look at that as an "intermediary" world,[1] a hybrid, whose ontology might be best grasped by way of a framework of theological understanding.[2]

Certainly, one part of our ability to see and hear is located clearly "on" the Web, where connectivity is quickly coming to be seen as a right, the violation of which has profound impact on people's social and relational capacities. Our very identity is more and more viewed as a conceptual value that becomes disseminated throughout various spaces and sites, rather than being simply and directly tied to who we are physically, that is, to our biological reality.

In the face of such considerations, Francis's response is both wise and courageous, because he does not simply theorize but takes a risk and pushes against the limits of our thinking:

It is not enough to be passersby on the digital highways, simply "connected"; connections need to grow into true encounters. We cannot live apart, closed in on ourselves. We need to love and to be loved. We need tenderness. Media strategies do not ensure beauty, goodness, and truth in communication. The world of media also has to be concerned with humanity; it too is called to show tenderness. The digital world can be an environment rich in humanity; a network not of wires but of people. The impartiality of media is merely an appearance; only those who go out of themselves in their communication can become a true point of reference for others. Personal engagement is the basis of the trustworthiness of a communicator. Christian witness, thanks to the Internet, can thereby reach the peripheries of human existence.

As I have frequently observed, if a choice has to be made between a bruised Church that goes out to the streets and a Church suffering from self-absorption, I certainly prefer the first. Those "streets" are the world where people live and where they can be reached, both effectively and affectively. The digital highway is one of them, a street teeming with people who are often hurting, men and women looking for salvation or hope. By means of the Internet, the Christian message can reach "to the ends of the earth" (Acts 1:8).[3]

In the Gospel parable about "neighbors," or as we might say today, our "contacts," the Levite and the priest "do not regard him in his reality as a neighbor, but instead see him through a 'pseudo-reality' as a stranger to be kept at a distance." And that is the danger nowadays, that "certain media establish 'rules' and 'rituals' that so condition our responses that we fail to see our real neighbor in order to seek out and serve other interests."[4]

The "rules" and "rituals" of Christianity are what give this point its validity: evangelization is not at all meant to signify "propagandizing" the Gospel. We are not simply "sending" messages of faith, because the Gospel is not merely one message among others. Hence, evangelization is not about simply "posting explicitly religious content" on Facebook or Twitter. Not to mention, the truth of the Gospel message does not derive from its popularity or the amount of attention it receives, how many "likes" it gets. On the contrary, the Pope emphasizes how necessary it is that we make ourselves available to the other men and women around us "by patiently and respectfully engaging their questions and their doubts as they advance in their search for the truth and the meaning of human existence."

To witness to our faith thus means, above all, to live an ordinary life that is nurtured by our faith in every way: worldview, choices, directions, tastes, and therefore, also, how we communicate, how we make friends and relate to others both online and off. As the Pope has written, we are called "to witness coherently, in our digital profile and in how we communicate, in our choices, preferences, and judgments such that they are consonant with the Gospel, even if that is not ever made explicit."[5] The online Church is called, therefore, not to be a "Web-based distributor of religious content" but rather to "share" the Gospel within a complex society. The Gospel is not merchandise to be sold within a "marketplace of ideas" saturated with information. Often a very discreet statement is all that is needed to spur another's interest or desire for greater truth or to influence another's conscience. In this way, one can avoid the trap of habitual and repetitive posting of content that people have already seen or heard. Effective witness ought to learn from the story of the Risen Christ meeting his disciples on the road to Emmaus (Luke 24:13-35), where the Lord came upon the two men, "their faces downcast," gently opening their hearts to a recognition of the mystery they were encountering.

The very fact that nowadays our connections to others can be separated from an experience of encounter, that sharing can be divorced from relationship, comes from the paradox that the Internet allows us to pursue relationships without our ever having to give up our prior condition of egotistical isolation. Sherry Turkle summed up this situation in the title of her book, *Alone Together* (New York: Basic Books, 2012). This lack of closeness comes from how technological mediation makes whoever happens to be "connected" to me my "neighbor."

What is the problem with this? The problem is that one may well find oneself "out of touch" with a friend who actually lives close by but isn't on Facebook or doesn't use email frequently and instead feel "close" to a person I have never met but who "friended" me and with whom I often chat online. This strange situation has its roots in the anonymity created by a mass society. Up until the beginning of the twentieth century, most people lived in a rural environment and knew perhaps only the hundred or so faces that they encountered in the course of their lives. Nowadays, the opposite is normal, that is, we hardly know anyone we see on the street, such that our neighbor is more or less a stranger to us. There is danger in a situation where we begin to think of our closeness to others using simplistic criteria that do not account for the true complexities inherent in a real relationship of depth.

Technology continues to train our brains to view our experience as if it were a video game based on a "right-answer/wrong-answer" paradigm in response to stimuli from our partners. For the Christian and anyone else, our neighbors most certainly are not those people who give us the "right answer" in response to what we do or say to them. The Gospel way is very clear in this regard:

> If you love those who love you, what credit is that to you? Even sinners love those who love them. And if you do good to those who are good to you, what credit is that to you? Even sinners do that. And if you lend to those from whom you expect repayment, what credit is that to you? Even sinners lend to sinners, expecting to be repaid in full. But love your enemies, do good to them, and lend to them without expecting to get anything back. Then your reward will be great, and you will be children of the Most High, because he is kind to the ungrateful and the wicked. (Luke 6:32-35)

When the Gospel writer Luke speaks of "doing good," we should understand him in the most literal way possible. Contact through online video games comes about primarily through "words," that is, story lines, written messages. Once upon a time, by contrast, young people could make friends only by *doing* things together, by sharing a hobby, going for pizza, playing in a band, taking part in a group. Nowadays, one can be "friends" by merely posting something on an online bulletin board.

8

Incarnation and Witness

To make friends, therefore, means dealing with a greater number of possibilities for contact, but it also requires a greater awareness of their intensity, of the depth that is only possible in an "incarnate" human relationship. And "incarnation," for Christians, is a concept essential to our physical experience of ourselves. Above all, it is witness to the greatest closeness available to us as human beings: Christ, who became flesh and dwelt among us. But it also means our closeness to those who suffer, who weep, as Pope Francis once again explains so well:

> Today we are living in a world that is growing ever "smaller" and where, as a result,

it would seem to be easier for all of us to be neighbors. Developments in travel and communications technology are bringing us closer together and making us more connected, even as globalization makes us increasingly interdependent. Nonetheless, divisions, which are sometimes quite deep, continue to exist within our human family. On the global level we see a scandalous gap between the opulence of the wealthy and the utter destitution of the poor. Often we need only walk the streets of a city to see the contrast between people living on the street and the brilliant lights of the store windows. We have become so accustomed to these things that they no longer unsettle us. Our world suffers from many forms of exclusion, marginalization, and poverty, to say nothing of conflicts born of a combination of economic, political, ideological, and, sadly, even religious motives.[1]

Thus, we understand how important both the notion and the practice of witnessing to our faith can be: it is a decisive aspect of who we are, particularly given how much credit we give to the opinions of others online. Nowadays, should I wish to get a sense of a particular book I might want to buy, I go online to a bookstore or to a social networking site for readers and I read the reviews. Likewise, if I want to buy music, or find a good restaurant, or a decent bed and breakfast. The examples these days are endless, and it all comes back to *user-generated content*, a concept central to the interactive world of the Internet.

This exchange of content, of course, is most effective and creates maximum "connection" when it occurs within a personal relationship, and this relational basis of knowledge is at the heart of the online world. Communication no longer happens by *broadcasting*, but rather by *sharing*, by involving the "listener" or the "audience," as we used to say.

Pope Francis, for example, does not just "communicate," but rather he creates "communication events," in which those who hear his message actively participate. Long before he was elected Pope, he practiced what he preached:

To be close to someone, moreover, always means to witness. Contrary to the ostensible neutrality of the media, only someone who engages his own ethics to bear and witnesses directly to the truth brings a point of view through which one might begin to see reality more clearly. His personal involvement is at the very heart of the trustworthiness of what he is communicating.[2]

Each one of us is called to assume our own measure of responsibility in the task of acquiring knowledge. In this way, Christians who live within social networks are called to commit themselves to a life of authenticity, for such a commitment bears directly on our capacity to communicate with others.

Information technology, by creating a network of connection, seems to tie the acquisition of knowledge even more tightly to the experience of friendship, leading us to bear "witness" to what our lives are based on. Nowadays, to communicate means to bear witness. Thus, any proclamation of the Gospel that is not based on the authenticity of one's everyday life, now more than ever, is a message coded in a way that might be understood with the mind but not with our hearts.

9

Church of Connections
or Mystical Body?

Given all these considerations concerning
what is means to be a "neighbor," how
might we imagine the future of our community
of faith in the Internet age? That well-known
observer of the mass media, Marshall McLuhan,
was right when he spoke of the magisterium of
the electronic age, noticing that conditions in
the twentieth century were similar to those of
the first decade of the Church:

There is, on the one hand, the immediacy
of interrelationship among Christians and
non-Christians alike in a world where
information moves at the speed of light.

The population of the world now co-exists in an extremely small space and in an instant of time. So far as the magisterium is concerned, it is as if the entire population were present in a small room where perpetual dialogue was possible.[1]

For quite some time now, encounters between people have often been mediated through technology: cars, buses, the telephone, and so forth. All these are technologies that make encounters with others—and even the sacraments—possible, and they are readily available to many and easy to access. Not so with regard to the more sophisticated digital technologies. Technological barriers to access ought to be considered as problematic as architectural barriers in construction, and they threaten to rob us of the opportunity to encounter differences in age, culture, work, ideas, and sensibilities in ways that might challenge us.

But a community cannot be governed absolutely, even by sophisticated technologies. Think of those communities of faith created by televangelism that reinforce a personal and private religious practice, a set of self-centered life goals, and the pursuit of an extreme individualism within a capitalist-consumer society, for which the motto "everyone for himself and God for all" might well be applied. It is not by mere chance that sites of a diffuse, New Age sort of spirituality, unconnected to any form of historical, community, or sacramental mediation (tradition, witness, celebration) are so successful, tending as they do to embrace all religious values according to one's own individual conscience.

And yet, that which appears to have been lost—the desire for physical contact with people and our friends—begins to be found in other ways and through other means. As we have already noted, the Internet is becoming less and less a parallel universe, separate and distinct from everyday life and direct encounters: the two dimensions of our life—online and offline—are more and more being pulled together, harmonized, and integrated into a life of genuine and fulfilling relationships. Under this rubric, the community of faith is becoming understood more (and is more understandable) in terms of a network.

And another fact is also very clear: the Church, in an Internet age of social networks, is called to appreciate the value, meaning, and forms of its online presence. I believe that it must embrace not just the mystery of communion it represents, but, even more humbly, the place of meaningful connection between people that it provides, so as to create, within a fragmented society, a basis for people to come together in relationships of communion with one another. In this fashion, we might apply the insights brought forward by theologians of an "emerging ecclesiology," like Dwight J. Friesen, Landon Whitsitt, Douglas Estes, Jesse Rice, and others, and apply these insights to our pastoral ministry, at least as a start.

One task, among others, before today's Church and its efforts at a "new evangelization" would therefore be to create a place for networking, where people might grow in faith and seek answers to their deepest questions within an atmosphere of meaningful relationship.

This task, evangelizing the Internet in an age of social networks, is complex but one quite congenial, I think, to Christians, who are called daily to transform mere contact into closeness. Each one of us can see, online, the "margins" to which we are called, crowded as they are with so many people waiting for and needing community.

Conclusion

To conclude, I'd like to summarize what has been said up to now in the form of six important challenges that the age of digital communication poses to the pastoral ministry of the Church, since, as Benedict XVI has written, "social networks are nourished by aspirations rooted in the human heart."[1] These challenges would require a change in perspective, a movement forward into the future while maintaining a respect for the past and the present. And they are the following:

1. A ministry that asks questions, rather than a ministry that provides answers.
2. A ministry centered around people, rather than a ministry focused on content.
3. A ministry of witness, rather than a ministry of transmission.

4. A ministry of neighborliness, rather than a ministry of propaganda.
5. A ministry of stories, rather than a ministry of ideas.
6. An interactive ministry attentive to interior life.

As for how to bring such a ministry about, one of the cardinal rules of Jesuit spirituality can be found in a saying of Ignatius of Loyola: "Seek and find God in all things." What we need to rediscover, therefore, is the knowledge encompassed by that venerable term of Christian spirituality: discernment. Spiritual discernment means recognizing which of the many important questions facing us is the most important, true, and fundamental. It is a complicated process that requires preparation and spiritual sensitivity. And it calls each of us Christians to synchronize—and to help others synchronize—the sophisticated functions of the digital technologies at our fingertips these days with the ancient and unequivocal call of the spiritual compass that points toward the north, and that we carry within each of us.

Notes

1 / Spiritual Technology

1. Paul VI, "Discorso al personale del 'Centro automazione analisi linguistica' dell'Aloisianum," June 19, 1964.
2. Benedict XVI, "Truth, Proclamation and Authenticity of Life in the Digital Age," Message for the 45th World Communications Day, January 24, 2011.
3. *Caritas in veritate,* no. 69.
4. Tom Beaudoin, *Virtual Faith: The Irreverent Spiritual Quest of Generation X* (San Francisco: Jossey-Bass, 1998), p. 87.
5. John Paul II, "Religion in the Mass Media," Message for 23rd World Communications Day, May 7, 1989.

2 / The Web and Relationships

1. Benedict XVI, "New Technologies, New Relationships: Promoting a Culture of Respect, Dialogue and Friendship," Message for the 43rd World Communications Day, May 24, 2009.

3 / The Internet Is a Real Place

1. With regard to the term "presence," which, as we will soon see, in the context of the Internet, will play a significant semantic role, we should not forget that the term is used in a very direct and literal way online: "if you don't post it, it doesn't exist." Today, among the 7 billion people in the world, only 40 percent have access to the Internet. The digital divide persists: 94 percent of those without access live in developing countries.

2. Benedict XVI, "Social Networks: Portals of Truth and Faith; New Spaces for Evangelization," Message for the 47th World Communications Day, May 12, 2013.

4 / Faith and Knowledge in the Age of the Internet

1. 2012 Synod of Bishops on New Evangelization, *Lineamenta*.

2. 2012 Synod of Bishops on New Evangelization, *Instrumentum laboris*.

3. A. Spadaro, *Cybertheology* (New York: Fordham University Press, 2014).

4. Benedict XVI, "Homily on the Solemnity of Pentecost," May 27, 2012.

5 / Not Just Connections but Communion

1. See L. De Carli. *Internet: Memoria e oblio* (Turin: Bollati Borlinghieri, 1997).

2. See C. Shirky, *Surplus cognitivo: Creatività e generosità nell'era digitale* (Turin: Codice, 2010).
3. *Catechism of the Catholic Church* (New York: Doubleday, 1995), p. 223n777.
4. *Lumen gentium*, no. 7.

6 / The Place of the Gift

1. Benedict XVI, in his extraordinary message for the 43rd World Communications Day in 2009.
2. Pope Francis, "Communicating the Family: A Privileged Place of Encounter with the Gift of Love," Message for the 49th World Communications Day, January 23, 2015.
3. Pope Francis, "Communication at the Service of a Culture of Encounter," Message for the 48th World Communications Day, June 1, 2014.

7 / Who Is Our Neighbor Online?

1. See P. Queau, *Metaxu: Théorie de l'art intermédiaire* (Seyssel: Champ Vallon, 1989).
2. See D. Herring, "Toward Sacrament in Cyberspace," *Epworth Review* 35 (2008): pp. 41-45.
3. Pope Francis, "Communication at the Service of a Culture of Encounter," Message for the 48th World Communications Day, June 1, 2014.
4. Ibid.
5. Benedict XVI, "Truth, Proclamation and Authenticity of Life in the Digital Age," Message for the 45th World Communications Day, January 24, 2011.

8 / Incarnation and Witness

1. Pope Francis, "Communication at the Service of a Culture of Encounter," Message for the 48th World Communications Day, June 1, 2014.
2. J. M. Bergoglio, "Comunicador, quién es tu prójimo?" in *La Nación*, Buenos Aires, October 10, 2002.

9 / Church of Connections or Mystical Body?

1. Marshall McLuhan, *The Medium and the Light: Reflections on Religion* (Eugene, OR: Wipf & Stock, 1999), p. 134.

Conclusion

1. Benedict XVI, "Social Networks: Portals of Truth and Faith; New Spaces for Evangelization," Message for the 47th World Communications Day, May 12, 2013.

Reflection Guide

Prepared by Daniella Zsupan-Jerome

Below are some suggested questions based on the content of each chapter. These can be used either for personal reflection or to guide a group discussion. The biblical passage and prayer for each chapter are additional suggestions if the reader seeks to reflect on these questions in a concretely prayerful setting.

Introduction

1. Recall a significant question that occurred to you or you have heard another ask. How was this question in itself "an opening through which God may still speak to us"? How do deep questions of faith invite us further into God's mystery?

Suggested Passage: Isaiah 58:2

Prayer

God of Mystery, the greatest questions of our lives are often also openings through which you speak to us. Living our lives in a digital culture we face great questions about knowing, being, and relating with one another. Send us your Spirit to illumine our way as we wade into mystery. We ask this in the name of Christ, the Word who reveals you to us by the breath of the Spirit. Amen.

1 / Spiritual Technology

1. Share a concrete example when technology has contributed to your "desire for meaning, truth, and unity."
2. How do you see technology being "created in our own image"?
3. How have you experienced social media as help for us "to answer God's call to form and to transform creation"?

Suggested Passage: Romans 8:18-27

Prayer

Creator God, you made us with the ability to invent, build, and make, we praise you for the wonders of technology as a sign of your creative work in us. These are not only the work of our hands but also expressions of who we are, made in your image. Send us your Spirit to fill our engagement with technology so that our own creativity may be our response to your call to form and transform creation. We ask this in the name of Christ, by the power of the Holy Spirit. Amen.

2 / The Web and Relationships

1. Can you share how specific relationships have become possible or have changed through your use of social media?
2. How ought one experience and react to hard-to-escape online exposure to advertising, violence, and pornography and the problem of privacy?
3. Have you had an experience when you clearly felt that social media engaged the deeper desires in your heart?

Suggested Passage: Ephesians 4:1-6

Prayer
Triune God, the mystery of your being is one of profound relationship. As Father, Son, and

Spirit, you are the ultimate meaning of relationship. We too, made in your image, are called to live relationally—with you, others, and indeed all of creation. Through the gift of technology we now live in an age where we experience the Internet as a social network. Teach us true relationship, one of participation, mutuality, and sharing so that we can indeed live out the Gospel online. We ask this in the name of your Son, by the power of the Spirit. Amen.

3 / The Internet Is a Real Place

1. Is the Internet a "real place" for you? Has it changed the way you live your days?
2. How has the Internet changed the conversations you are having with colleagues, friends, and family? Can you share a few examples?
3. Are you different when relating to others in real and in virtual space? Do you feel comfortable with your "online persona"? Do you experience a difference in tone from others when they are or are not online?

Suggested Passage: John 1:1-14

Prayer

God-With-Us, contemplating your mystery we discover your presence in all that is real, true, and authentic. Your sent your Son to dwell among us, and his Real Presence remains with us in the life of your Church, his Body. Send us your Spirit so that we can recognize and practice real presence in and through digital culture and open our eyes to how words, signs, and images on the screen may reveal more fully to us the real presence of others. We ask this in the name of Christ, by the power of the Holy Spirit. Amen.

4 / Faith and Knowledge in the Age of the Internet

1. What is your understanding of the term cybertheology (p. 29)? How might this term be relevant to your community?
2. How does the Internet provide an opportunity for your faith to seek understanding?
3. How can you/your community increase the understanding between people rather than just adding "noise" to others' lives via the Internet?

Suggested Passage : 1 Kings 3:10-14

Prayer

All-Knowing God, our faith seeks understanding as you draw us ever deeper into your mystery. Your grace gives us eyes to perceive the world as replete with symbols of your presence. Grant us your grace to continue to discover how the Internet too can lead us to greater understanding of your mystery as well, not just as a technology, but as a context that reveals more about you and ourselves and one another. Grant this through Christ the Word who speaks to us in old ways and new. Amen.

5 / Not Just Connections but Communion

1. How do you understand the two terms "connection" and "communion"? How do you see these two as related?
2. How have you experienced friendship online? What does it mean to "friend" someone on a platform like Facebook? How does this compare with a broader understanding of friendship?

3. "The challenge, therefore, is not how we should "use" the Internet, as one often hears, but rather how to "live well" in the Internet age" (p. 34). What does this mean to you?

Suggested Passage: John 15:11-17

Prayer

Most Holy Trinity, the mystery of your being reveals perfect divine communion between Father, Son, and Holy Spirit. All of our ways of relating with one another, including digital communication, are ordered toward this ultimate mystery. Shape us so that our connections with one another may grow toward communion, and that we may reach always toward communion as we reach out to others. Although we are imperfect, teach us perfection as we contemplate your way of mutuality, self-gift, and reciprocal love. We ask this in the name of Jesus Christ, the Perfect Communicator, who draws us into your mystery in friendship and love. Amen.

6 / The Place of the Gift

1. Think about your own experience of communication in your family. What does the family teach us about communication? Why might the church use the family as a paradigm for "correct communication" (p. 42)?
2. What is the meaning of "gift" in our digital culture? How does this compare with the understanding of "gift" in Christian thought (pp. 42–43)? What can we learn from this for our ways of being online?
3. Share from your understanding and experience of online "neighborliness."

Suggested Passage: Luke 10:29-37

Prayer

Generous God, we hold up our empty, open hands to you to receive daily the gifts that you freely and lovingly bestow on us. In being gifted by you, we in turn become gifts of your love and blessing to those around us. Guide us to be generous and self-giving in our communication, especially in times of conflict, violence, or injustice. May our words always tend the wounds of those left wounded by the side of the road. We ask this through Christ the Word, by the breath of the Spirit. Amen.

7 / Who Is Our Neighbor Online?

1. How do you understand "social presence"? Can you share experiences of Internet "presence" that had an impact on you?
2. What does it mean to truly encounter another person online? How does this compare with truly encountering a person face-to-face?
3. Have you seen moments of "tenderness" online? What moved you about them?

Suggested Passage: Luke 24:13-35

Prayer

Faithful God, you are with us until the end of the age. Awaiting the fullness of your Kingdom, we persist in hope as we experience both your presence and your absence in our midst. Encourage us to seek true encounters in and through digital culture, and to walk with one another as we seek meaning and understanding, especially during our darkest times. May we find communion and your real presence in places we gather as one. We ask this through the Risen Christ, by the power of the Spirit. Amen.

8 / Incarnation and Witness

1. What does it mean to be a "witness" to the faith? How can we "witness" authentically online?
2. Where in cyberspace do you see temptations not to be authentic? What is the antidote?
3. "Communication no longer happens by broadcasting but rather by sharing, by involving the listener or audience" (p. 57). What does this mean for the Christian's call to proclaim the Gospel? What might evangelization look like online?

Suggested Passage: Mark 16:14-20

Prayer
God of Salvation, your Son commissioned his followers to go and proclaim the Gospel to every creature. We too seek to follow this great commission, and to make present your

good news now in digital culture. Send us your Spirit so that we can do this joyfully, authentically, and creatively, offering words, deeds, and a witness of life that reveal your saving word for all. Grant this through Christ the Word by the breath of the Spirit. Amen.

9 / Church of Connections or Mystical Body?

1. How do you understand "the community of faith" today? How does digital culture offer the possibility for gathering with others in faith? How does this challenge enhance our physical, local gatherings as church?
2. How is the Church both a "mystery of communion" and also "place of meaningful connection between people" (p. 63)? Why does this matter for digital culture?
3. According to Spadaro, one task of the new evangelization is "to create a place for networking, where people might grow in faith and seek answers to their deepest questions within an atmosphere of meaningful relationship" (p. 63). What do you think?

Suggested Passage: Romans 12:1-8

Prayer

Almighty God, through your Son we are made one as members of his Body. As the Church, we are a people gathered as a community of faith that lives and shares your good news of salvation. Your Spirit, which gives life to this Body, also prompts us to ever-new ways to love and serve in the name of your Son in the world today. May your Spirit guide us to be a true community in the digital age, and to offer hope, joy, and meaning especially to those on the margins. We ask this in the name of Jesus the Word by the breath of the Spirit. Amen.

10 / Conclusion

1. Consider Spadaro's six points about the pastoral ministry of the Church in a digital age. (pp. 65–66) Which of these do you resonate with the most? Which of these holds the greatest challenge for you?
2. Why might spiritual discernment be an essential part of engaging digital culture?

3. What is your greatest hope for "friending God" in our digital age?

Suggested Passage: Hebrews 4:12-16

Prayer

God our Hope, we trust in your grace especially in times of great change, such as the one we are living today. Like you, the Internet is a mystery, but we are too close to it to see yet where we are headed. At the same time we trust in the movement of your creative and life-giving Spirit to imbue and animate us in this worldly mystery so that it would become the context where we approach communion, a space where we engage in true encounter, a network for authentic community. Bless our communication and allow us to conform ever more closely to the image of your Son, the Word Incarnate and the Perfect Communicator of your good news. We ask this in his name, trusting in the Holy Spirit. Amen.

About the Author

Antonio Spadaro, S.J., was born in Messina, Italy, in 1966. He received an early classical education, followed by philosophical and theological studies. His philosophical training was at the University of Messina and the "Aloisianum" Institute in Padua. His theological education at the Pontifical Theological Faculty of Southern Italy, Pontifical Urban University, and the Pontifical Gregorian University led to degrees in theology (bachelor of theology, licentiate in theology, and doctorate in theology) and in social communications (diploma in social communications).

He has taught at the Massimilio Massimo Institute in Rome, the Pontano Institute in Naples, and the Pontifical Gregorian Institute in Rome.

His scholarly interests are in the areas of literature and literary criticism, particularly as they relate to Italian and American writers, music, contemporary art, and new communication technologies and their impact on culture.

He was ordained a priest in 1996 and is a member of the Society of Jesus (Jesuits), having professed solemn vows in 2007.

In addition to his current teaching and extensive involvement in social communication, he is editor of *La civiltà cattolica*.

About the Author of the Reflection Guide

Daniella Zsupan-Jerome, Ph.D., is professor of pastoral theology at Notre Dame Seminary Graduate School of Theology in New Orleans, LA. She holds a bachelor's degree in theology from the University of Notre Dame, a master's degree in liturgy from St. John's University in Collegeville, MN, a master's degree in religion and the arts from Yale Divinity School, and a Ph.D. in theology and education from Boston College. Her research focuses on social communication and ministry, especially digital culture and its potential for faith formation. She serves as a consultant for the United States Conference of Catholic Bishops' Committee on Communication and is author of the book *Connected Toward Communion: The Church and Social Communication in the Digital Age*

(Collegeville, MN: Liturgical Press, 2014). She has also published a number of articles and devotional resources, including Liturgy Training Publication's Daily Prayer 2013, Arts and Faith Advent and Lent from Loyola Press, and regularly contributes to Liturgical Press's Give Us This Day series.

About the Translator

ROBERT H. HOPCKE is the author of numerous works in the field of Jungian psychology and Roman Catholic spirituality. He has translated a variety of books in fields as diverse as art history, sexuality, and religion, including most recently, with Paul A. Schwartz, *The Little Flowers of St. Francis*, from Shambhala Publications.

About the Publisher

The CROSSROAD PUBLISHING COMPANY publishes CROSSROAD and HERDER & HERDER books. We offer a 200-year global family tradition of books on spiritual living and religious thought. We promote reading as a time-tested discipline for focus and understanding. We help authors shape, clarify, write, and effectively promote their ideas. We select, edit, and distribute books. With our expertise and passion we provide wholesome spiritual nourishment for heart, mind, and soul through the written word.

Additional Reading

Leonardo Boff
TOWARD AN ECO-SPIRITUALITY
Church at the Crossroad Series

An action plan, based on Christianity, to study and understand the challenges and ramifications of the global ecological crisis. Known as one of the major liberation theologians, Leonardo Boff has long seen the terrible cost of the ecological crisis to the poor. In this engaging brief, he outlines a new vision for human stewardship of the earth. This is an ideal first step to take for individuals and groups to study ecology in a Christian context, and to understand that ecology is no longer a luxury for a few, but an imperative for everyone working for a more just world

Paperback, 80 pages, 978-0-8245-2076-2

Oscar Andres Rodriquez Maradiaga
THE CHALLENGE OF INEQUALITY
Church at the Crossroad Series

A truly Christian perspective on global economic inequality from a prominent Cardinal and close ally of Pope Francis. In this treatise, author Cardinal Rodriguez-Maradiaga offers a clear analysis of the expansion of economic inequality and its root causes, followed by a review of suggested solutions, and a hopeful outlook based on a new model of economic and human growth. Maradiaga is one of the most outspoken members of the Catholic hierarchy when it comes to the growing inequality around the world. As one of the Church's most informed experts on social issues, Maradiaga holds that it is imperative for any Christian community to look at the dire state of social justice in the world, and to work for positive change. However, to do so requires a clear understanding of the issues at hand, and a comprehensive practice based on the laws of ethics.

Paperback, 76 pages, 978-0-8245-2081-6

Support your local bookstore or order
directly from the publisher at www.crossroadpublishing.com.
To request a catalog or inquire about
quantity orders, e-mail sales@crossroadpublishing.com.

The Crossroad Publishing Company

Additional Reading

Philip Jenkins
THE NEW MAP OF THE GLOBAL CHURCH
Church at the Crossroad Series

Offers an inviting way to understand the facts and implications of the major demographic shifts happening within Christianity. By 2025, 75 percent of Catholics in the world will be non-European; the new global church will have its center of gravity in Latin America, Asia, and Africa. This fascinating brief explores the metamorphosis taking place in the global community of believers: the church's new life comes from what historically has been labeled the periphery. The book also looks into the radical ramifications for all churches.

Paperback, 100 pages, 978-0-8245-2078-6

Diego Fares, S.J.
THE HEART OF POPE FRANCIS
*How a New Culture of Encounter Is Changing
the Church and the World*

The culture of encounter is like a map to the thoughts and feelings of Pope Francis. At the heart of his vision lies a keen interest in people, a passion for understanding the life experience of the other. By reaching out, welcoming, and listening to others, especially those at the margins, Pope Francis has already changed the Church more than we might even understand.

Paperback, 112 pages, 978-0-8245-2074-8

*Support your local bookstore or order
directly from the publisher at www.crossroadpublishing.com.
To request a catalog or inquire about
quantity orders, e-mail sales@crossroadpublishing.com.*

The Crossroad Publishing Company